The Academic Vampire

Rajen Akalu

Cover art: *Perseus and Andromeda* by Titian (1485 - 1576)

ISBN 979-8-3985-8777-7

CONTENTS

Introduction

We live in a time and age when knowledge is abundant and wisdom is scarce. Nowhere is this more evident than in the modern university. The reasons for the current state of affairs are both numerous and varied, and without a clear sense of what went wrong or how, it is difficult to see a way forward. While we may not have the answers, we can develop the courage to ask questions bravely. Part of the problem, however, is that the range of acceptable opinions, public or academic, has become far narrower than before. The kinds of questions we are prepared to ask have become more limited.

We sometimes shy away from research inquiries and discussions on contentious issues in order not to offend anyone or be singled out for having an unorthodox viewpoint. We say nothing, hoping that the controversy will pass and resolve itself in due course, or we seek like-minded individuals that share our own views (and biases). These intellectual pathologies plague academics, the university institutions they work at, the students they graduate and society in general. Unchallenged, our viewpoints become impediments to our own learning as we no longer have a solid foundation for our beliefs and are unable to act with any resolve.

Since we all learn by stories, it is by telling and retelling the stories that animate our culture and permeate our collective consciousness that we overcome our intellectual paralysis and become motivated to take the necessary action required to promote our highest ideals. This is a story about an assistant professor (who is a vampire) who has an affair with his graduate student. The student gets pregnant and has an abortion. This sets the stage to examine a range of ethical issues such as feminism, the "Me Too" movement, gender identity, Black Lives Matter, artificial intelligence, technological progress as well as the limits of secularism in academic research.

Fiction is somehow a more appropriate vehicle to communicate truth here because it requires a suspension of belief. This allows the ideas to be explored without the individual becoming identified or otherwise attached to them. The aim is to get back to examining and defending ideas honestly and fairly. One of the best ways to iron out the kinks in your thinking is through dialogue.

Sadly, in a world of misinformation, alternative facts, fake news, deep fakes and extremist views, having a reasonably held difference of opinion can be career limiting, resulting in social ostracism or online attacks. What seems more important than truth is that we look like we all get along and everyone feels comfortable. The polarizing effect this has had on public discourse is experienced most acutely on social media and the internet. Pundits and gurus emerge to fill the void left by reasonable people and our social problems become more precipitous and calamitous. Students coddled by safe-spaces find themselves intellectually cornered and unable to defend their ideas.

My hope is that these dialogues will help stimulate your thinking, challenge your beliefs, and we will both become stronger in the process.

The Two-Body Hire

This dialogue occurs between two seasoned academics, Anthony Moliere and Ursula Pastors, at the start of term. Both are well-respected researchers that have been hired by a new university to bolster the institution's credibility. What is not known to the university is that Anthony and Ursula are both vampires. They have been feeding off graduate students for blood since the mid-seventeenth century. It used to be the case that people never really noticed the odd grad student or two go missing from an international academic conference. Now the university administration has "Highly Qualified Personnel" as a performance metric for professors. As such, graduate students are tracked and need to be accounted for.

URSULA: Do you think we'll be happy here?

ANTHONY: Happy? What's happiness got to do with it? We've been to so many universities at this point, how will this one be any different?

URSULA: But aren't you looking forward to the start of term?

ANTHONY: Yes. The students are what prevent us from drying up.

URSULA: Not only that, you have to admit they're fun to be around, so wide-eyed and eager to learn.

ANTHONY: Which century are you referring to, Ursula? Sure, there was a time when research and scholarship meant something — now all that happens is students come to campus to get infected with bad ideas and then sent into the world to corrupt it.

URSULA: Really, Anthony, that's over dramatic even for you.

ANTHONY: Is it, Ursula? This afternoon I got an email from the Office of Research Services calling for proposals for 'Womxn' research.

URSULA: What's that?

ANTHONY: It's the PC inclusive term for persons that self-identify as trans or non-binary. This has nothing to do with research, you just have to claim you have womxn status and you'll be practically thrown grant money. It's complete nonsense. Diversity, Inclusion and Equity. Is it any wonder that the acronym spells D.I.E?

URSULA: Okay, I get you don't like the trend, but that doesn't mean it's not valid. It's important to have a diversity of voices in academia.

ANTHONY: There is a medical term for a diversity of voices in your head. That term is schizophrenia. If you want to write about your 'lived experience,' write a goddamn journal. If you want to see yourself reflected in something, buy a mirror. Who cares how many of the faculty identify as black lesbians? Or if you're non-binary? How many acronyms do you actually need to express your sexual orientation anyway?

URSULA: But don't you think it's better to create safe spaces on campus, where students are free to express themselves? It wasn't that long ago that you could go to prison for being gay. We've become more open, more tolerant, more accepting of differences and that's a good thing.

ANTHONY: There is a difference between being open-minded and empty-headed, you can't just wave the rainbow flag around, say 'love is love is love' and expect everything to be OK; it won't be. Students graduate having less idea of who or what they are, what to aim for or to aspire to be like. The creation of 'safe spaces' is having the paradoxical effect of making everyone overly sensitive and more fragile.

URSULA: Actually, we shouldn't forget members of the trans community, they have their own flag, you know.

ANTHONY: Don't get me started with all that gender fluid nonsense — there are two biological sexes, male and female; why should we change everything for a fraction of the population that doesn't feel comfortable with what they are?

URSULA: It's more complicated than that, what we regard as male and female are just social constructs. They don't define everyone's experience and they reinforce the dominant hegemony, one where white men are on top and the contributions of others are not valued.

ANTHONY: I was wondering when you were going to bring race into the mix — white privilege, isn't it?

URSULA: What's wrong with drawing attention to the fact that white people have it easier than other races because of historical advantages and slavery?

ANTHONY: What's wrong with it is that it's wrong! It's wrong to reduce people to their racial identities — that's racist! I have no problem discussing specific individuals that happen to be white and also are privileged. Justin Trudeau is a case in point. There is no way that Trudeau would have become prime minister if it were not for his family name or connections. It doesn't matter if you're liberal or conservative, there would be white people on both sides of the political spectrum that would agree with that statement. People are more than their skin tone or ethnicity. Somehow we seem to have forgotten this. Why do we think it's OK to lower university admission standards to accommodate racial groups with perceived historical disadvantages?

URSULA: Well, isn't it good to have a diverse campus body?

ANTHONY: Diversity of thought and ideas, yes, diversity of races and genders, hell no. What's with diversity anyway? It's a unicorn; no one has ever actually seen it, but everyone believes that it will somehow make everything OK. 'Diversity is our strength,' and so on. But no one bothers to ask for evidence that diversity actually improves anything. Diversity isn't a place you arrive at, it's a set of circumstances that we have to figure out how to overcome. Lowering admission standards and setting quotas based on current demographic trends will only serve to breed resentment, envy and distrust of institutions, academic or otherwise. No good can come of this.

URSULA: But what about Black Lives Matter?

ANTHONY: What about black lives? How are they any more or less important than anyone else? Either all lives matter or no individual life does.

URSULA: But you have to admit black people are more likely to be profiled by the police and sent to jail; they've suffered years of historical oppression and systemic racism.

ANTHONY: Are you seriously claiming that racism toward black people is worse now than it was fifty years ago? That entire race could easily be lifted out of their socio-economic status in one or two generations if black people married before they carried. You can't tell me that the system creates baby daddies and baby mamas. If Snoop Dogg and Tupac are your role models, what do you expect to happen? You can't tell me that the police are profiling seven-year-old black children because they might commit a crime sometime in the future. When you don't take responsibility, someone else will get power over you. That's not systemic anything, that's just reality. You can struggle against it, you can pretend it doesn't exist, you can make excuses, but nothing will change unless you change first.

URSULA: So you don't think that certain races have advantages over others? You have to admit that it's easier for a white person to get ahead.

ANTHONY: So you're back to white privilege again. This is Canada — if you live in Canada, you have privilege over someone living in Yemen! No one is telling you to cover up if you're a woman and that you can't sleep with a man if you're a man. You have those rights and freedoms, what people forget however is that freedom comes with the responsibility to make personal choices that are aligned with human flourishing. It doesn't mean you're entitled to do whatever you want whenever you want and everyone else just has to put up with it. Any social arrangement will disadvantage someone. Some people are smarter and work harder than others. Isn't society better off if those talented people occupy positions of power and authority in our society? Are some people in positions of power racist, homophobic or transphobic? Yes. Do some of those people happen to be white? Sure, but that doesn't mean that racism is systemic. Cream rises to the top

URSULA: I think you're revealing your unconscious bias. Why would you use the metaphor of cream? You make an implicit association that white is better than others; why else would you refer to cream, that's precisely the kind of thinking that needs to be challenged.

ANTHONY: You've got to be kidding Ursula, you're playing CRT semantics now. The pandemic in academia right now is critical race theory with its overtly racist invective masquerading as virtue. Students have become so terrified of offending anyone they don't say anything important at all. They can't defend their ideas because they're too busy coddling themselves and each other. But the problem is the truth is necessarily offensive to those that lie and reality tends to be a problem for those that are delusional.

URSULA: I don't think you're being fair. Some people have it hard through no fault of their own. You can't expect equality of opportunity when the odds are stacked against you. You have to admit that the institutions benefit the dominant classes — individuals and groups that have the resources and networks to bias the outcomes in their favour. What's wrong with pointing that out? Assisting people at the bottom. The people on top aren't necessarily going to do that of their own accord. Don't you want to live in a world that values equity?

ANTHONY: No. I want to live in a world that values merit. I don't really care what race or gender you are as long as you're competent. Is that really too much to ask?

URSULA: The problem with the current merit paradigm is that it reinforces the dominant hegemony. Only people that are already at the top will meet the standard. The ladder is kicked away for everyone else.

ANTHONY: So what, you have a problem with standards now? News flash: all systems of testing are biased! An exam written in an English-speaking country will generally be written in English unless that exam is testing another language. That automatically will put Chinese students at a disadvantage. It would simply be unworkable to have every student write a test in their preferred language.

URSULA: I don't have a problem with standards, just the ones that result in inequality.

ANTHONY: How can you expect equality of outcome when intelligence is unevenly distributed and no one starts life at exactly the same point as everyone else? It doesn't make a difference whether you're talking about race or gender or any other social grouping for that matter. There will always be smart and not so smart people. People born into good and bad families or favourable or unfavourable circumstances. The problem isn't so much realizing some cosmetic version of diversity, but rather overcoming the challenges brought about by people having varying levels of ability, motivations and relative positions.

URSULA: So what you're saying is that some people are good for nothing.

ANTHONY: No, I am saying that there are some people who are not good for anything that anyone would be willing to pay them for. That's not the same as nothing. Your problem is that you only want to look at the people on the top and you ask, why more people that are 'diverse' aren't getting there. You seem to ignore that there are a lot of people at the bottom that no one seems to care who they are.

URSULA: I don't think you're getting my point, it's more about celebrating the abilities and talents of others. Leveling the playing field so to speak.

ANTHONY: I think we're not watching the same game, Ursula. Life isn't an Olympic sport where you can control all the variables and let the best player win. The field of life is seldom ever a level playing field. Where you are born is as much to do with chance than anything else. Since people are endowed with varying levels of ability and intellect, the equality that you are advancing is an abstraction based on your own personal bias on what is 'right or fair.'

URSULA: Actually, we decide as a society what is right or fair. That is implemented through public policy.

ANTHONY: Dress it up however you like. Public policy is by definition teleological. The telos is the end point or objective to be implemented. In this case, it is some vague notion of justice that is putatively expedited via social reform. Reformer types make the mistake that objects of reform are resources — human resources. The problem with that is that people are not lumber. They have hopes and aspirations, goals and motivations. They won't necessarily respond to a government mandate that limits their self-interest for the greater good without a compelling moral justification. A quota of diverse people in positions of power is not a compelling moral justification.

URSULA: So what is?

ANTHONY: Competence, for a start. People should be competent in the work that they do. It doesn't matter where they're from. Do some people get breaks? Do some people have it easier than others? Undoubtedly. But the answer isn't starting again and redistributing everything equally. Lowering admission standards hurts everyone, particularly the people you are supposedly trying to help. What we need to be doing is improving one student at a time so they can meet the required standard and be recognized for that. What we are doing now is simply qualifying a person's accomplishment in ways that are based on preconceived notions of the barriers they face based on an arbitrarily assigned social group. That's just bigotry disguised as justice — social justice.

URSULA: So you don't believe in social justice, then.

ANTHONY: No. There's justice or injustice. Once you start qualifying justice, you introduce arbitrariness and ambiguity that didn't exist before. You can no longer rely on the rule of law because there are no rules — or at least no rules you can predictably rely on. You can't arrive at some socialist utopia just by slapping the word social on the word justice. All you are doing is making things confusing. But that is the point. If things are confusing, someone needs to be there to clean up the mess that gets created. Biasing an outcome without understanding the specific facts is bound to create problems. Social justice is simply prejudice, by another name.

URSULA: So you're saying people should not fight oppression? The way it is, is just the way it is and we should just all accept it, no matter how unfair the outcomes are? How are we supposed to effect social reform without addressing the systemic issues at the institutional level?

ANTHONY: Well that depends on how you define institutions and what you think they are for. The best definition of an institution that I've ever seen was from JR Commons. He defined institutions as 'collective action in control, liberation and expansion of individual action.'

URSULA: Nobody cares what Commons had to say, he was a racist. He wrote *Immigrants and Races in America* which conveniently put Whites on top and Blacks on the bottom.

ANTHONY: Even if JR Commons was a racist, does it make his contribution to the study of institutions any less valid? This is my problem, everyone thinks that they can rewrite history and put themselves on the right side of it. If you said the wrong thing at some point, then you're cancelled and erased. Nothing you ever said was valuable. History is not inscrutable, but it's not malleable either. This is how ethics becomes relative. This is how we lose our way. We end up pulling down statutes instead of learning from the accomplishments and the failings of the people that they memorialize. No one is perfect.

URSULA: Get over yourself, everything looks better when you're on top. It's easy to say, 'well that's just the way it is' when you're sitting on top. The view looks very different from the bottom.

ANTHONY: If you were not a vampire, I would almost believe that you are sincere in your argument.

URSULA: [laughing] Yes, I can't deny the grads we had lately are a lot less salty...Let's get going. I have an orientation event this afternoon.

The Library Archive

Anthony takes a trip to the library archives to visit an old librarian friend, Eva Cortez. Like Anthony, Eva is a vampire. As a librarian she has spent many years in the library archives. Like most librarians she is agreeable and service oriented. She particularly loves helping members of the public at the circulation desk. Although she feels bad about killing, she accepts this as a necessity to sustain herself. Her strategy is to lay waiting in the archives for her prey, usually overly ambitious research assistants. Although she enjoys the taste of blood, she often apologizes as the life drains from her victims. Eva has been a vampire longer than Anthony. She began her career at the oldest university in the world, the University of Bologna in Italy. The pair discuss the origin and evolution of the university. Their discussion centers on whether faith is the foundation of intellectual community.

EVA: So great to see you!

ANTHONY: You too. How long has it been?

EVA: Definitely pre-Enlightenment.

ANTHONY: Really? So much has changed since then. We've made so much progress.

EVA: I'm not too sure about that. We can't even define what a woman is anymore, that's hardly progress.

ANTHONY: OK. I agree with you on that. The gender fluidity nonsense has induced a form of institutional psychosis at the university. People that I've known for years are now stating their preferred pronouns in their email signature. You're a mother of two and your name is Betsy. I'm not sure what putting 'She/her' in your email signature accomplishes other than to indicate you're a virtue-signaling cipher.

EVA: Hey, I do that. But only because you're going to get singled out otherwise. Plus, what's wrong about being in support of the current thing? Your face! Ha. It's so easy to get under your skin. No wonder Ursula has stayed with you all these years. But seriously, we're vampires, we have to blend in otherwise people will get suspicious.

ANTHONY: Yeah, I wonder why I bother with it when it's so much easier just to go along. So why do you think we haven't made much progress? We have a better standard of living. People are living longer, living healthier. We have the internet now. We've entered the information age.

EVA: We've made material progress certainly. But the academic soul has become emaciated in the process. Pluralism and secularism have divorced faith and religion in the academic enterprise. The academic mission has veered away from freedom and truth toward intellectual enslavement and pandering to interest groups. This is the deep moral crisis of the postmodern university.

ANTHONY: You'll need to unpack that for me; I'm not sure I follow.

EVA: Well, the university as an institution of higher education is the product of Christian culture. While it may not be politically correct to say this, it is very much the case. I started out at the University of Bologna. That university was founded in 1088 A.D. Back then all research needed to have its origin in scripture. Universities grew out of monastic orders and libraries blossomed with the advent of Gutenberg's printing press in 1436.

ANTHONY: I'm not sure I buy that. Christianity, like all religion, relies on myth. The leap of faith. This faith is promoted as a virtue when really it has been a vice. It has resulted in untold suffering and wars. Look at how the Catholic priests abused children and set up the residential schools. You think our scientific understanding grew out of that? If anything, religion has impeded scientific progress. At some point you realize Father Christmas doesn't exist. Besides, what makes Christianity any different from any other religion anyway?

EVA: Ever young and foolish Anthony. You really need to spend less time trying to predict the future and instead learn something from the accumulated wisdom of the past. The founder of the scientific method, Francis Bacon, was a devout Anglican. His approach promoted scientific experimentation as a way of glorifying God, relieving man's estate and fulfilling scripture. Bacon was vehemently opposed to atheism. He remarked that a little philosophy inclines man's mind to atheism, but depth in philosophy brings men's minds about to religion. You, my friend, are a case in point.

ANTHONY: But you have to admit that the Bible has been interpreted to restrain rather than liberate people. It's a tool that the dominant classes use to oppress everyone else.

EVA: You have a little too much Marx in your diet, Anthony. Religion is not the opiate of the masses; it sustains the individuals that constitute society. Witness the demons of depression and anxiety that emerge in its absence. Our science and culture flows downstream from religion. In the absence of religion, academics end up establishing idols of the mind. They become overly obsessed with metrics that do not matter to prove points no one cares about. The intellectual pursuit of truth unmoored from its moral and religious underpinnings creates a multiversity — academic silos discussing their discipline using increasingly abstruse terms. What tends to be forgotten is the word discipline has its etymology in the Latin 'discipulus,' meaning pupil. The concept developed from the disciples or followers of Jesus Christ during his lifetime. Christ as the embodiment of Truth as symbolized by the cross was the focal point to which all research questions and indeed all human endeavors were to be aimed.

ANTHONY: But surely no one believes that now.

EVA: When enough people orient themselves away from truth, they are easily deceived because their internal condition is not well-ordered. Chaos is around the corner. At some point society will go into free fall. Lies reign when no one wants to tell the truth.

ANTHONY: You can't be serious. You don't need a 2,000-year-old superstition or a belief in a bearded guy in the sky in order to do science or to know to tell the truth.

EVA: Really now? Are you sure? What difference does it make what we do if there's no God? If there's no God, there's no right or wrong. Those categories are irrelevant. Without a belief in an immaterial transcendent creator, nothing makes sense. There's no university because there's no universal truth. Everything devolves into relativism as a series of random unconnected facts of no consequence whatsoever.

ANTHONY: That's not true. Human beings have evolved to have reason and the ability to act rationally.

EVA: Darwinian evolution is a scientific theory. No theory in science is immutable since every field of human knowledge is tentative, provisional and corrigible. Theories are not valueless of course; they enable us to participate in a shared illusion that allows us to interact with each other. Language and money are prime examples of this. They are the great inventions of humanity as they allow us to communicate and exchange with each other. But they are ultimately abstractions that serve a symbolic and semiotic function. They have no intrinsic value. When we lose sight of this, the shared illusion becomes a shared delusion.

ANTHONY: But there's an overwhelming scientific consensus on Darwin's theory. It's all been empirically confirmed by practically everyone. You're going to tell me that the earth is flat next.

EVA: The world is too perfect to have been created by chance. The theory of evolution is for the intellectually indolent; it ascribes randomness to anything that is unknown. Many theories once thought iron-clad have since been debunked. Prior to the Copernican revolution and the heliocentric model with the Sun at the centre of the Solar System, everyone believed the Earth was stationary and at the centre of the universe. Man is more than a highly evolved amoeba, wouldn't you say?

ANTHONY: Yes. We have logic and reason and this separates us from lower organisms. This allows us to make laws that govern ourselves and engage in scientific research.

EVA: If what you're saying is true then the government of the day or scientific consensus is essentially God, since it is the final authority beyond which there is no appeal. I have less faith in politicians or scientists. They are becoming increasingly indistinguishable from each other these days in any event. What's popular is what's right and what's right is what's popular. That's the problem with consensus, it often obscures the truth.

ANTHONY: But your way of thinking relies on something that has no proof.

EVA: What proof would satisfy you? If Jesus Christ showed up today, he would be immediately dismissed as fake news. You operate on the assumption that seeing is believing but it is in fact the opposite that is true. Believing is seeing. What we expect is framed by what we believe. Without this lens of perception human beings would not be able to filter out extraneous information, prioritize choices and take action. Science only enables methodological observation of matter, meaning – what matters is found through Jesus Christ.

ANTHONY: Are you saying that Christianity is better than other religions?

EVA: That depends on what you mean by better. Every religion can be judged by the culture it has produced since cultures flow downstream from a society's religion. The religion of any society represents its highest ideal. You would be hard pressed to find a society more tolerant and economically prosperous than the ones that have been based on Judeo-Christian ideals. Modern science would not be the same without Christianity. Indeed our experience of time would not be the same.

ANTHONY: Time?

EVA: Every cheque you have ever written, every contract you have ever signed will have a date. That date is a reference to Christ. The calendar that the world uses today, the Gregorian Calendar, was settled in 1582 by Pope Gregory. It was in this year that the astronomical observations of Kepler were incorporated to recalibrate the inaccuracies of the Julian Calendar. This is why we have leap years. We forget that A.D. after the date takes after the Latin *Anno Domini*, the year of our Lord. We instead focus on the efficiencies and the material benefits that come with quantifying and commodifying time. However, we lose our religion in the process, becoming slaves to time rather than followers of Christ. This is a modern problem and it is a pattern that gets repeated again and again in the biblical narrative. We turn away from God rather than toward Him. Eventually we suffer the consequences. Every generation has to learn and relearn this. The time and date is a prime example of scientific discovery and religious truth. There are many other calendars from various cultures and religions, but the date and time developed by Christians is the most widely used. Without an agreed date and accurate time-keeping modern technology simply wouldn't work. The text message you sent when you arrived could not be routed via cell towers, satellites could not be coordinated so your GPS would not work. Secular academics generally don't like hearing about the role Christ plays in their lives. Everyone, certainly everyone in the West, owes something to Christ. Unfortunately, many want the gifts that come with Christmas, without participating in the suffering of Christ. Most people have no problem making land acknowledgements recognizing indigenous treaty lands. Such vapid sentiments are almost entirely self-serving and devoid of any meaning. They allow people to feel good about themselves while they continue to do what they have always done. Most people would much rather engage in this nauseating charade of virtue signaling than acknowledge Christ. It is not without good reason of course, standing up for truth as it will put you at odds with those that are comfortable with deceit. This is lamentable since suffering in Christ's name is the best that can be accomplished with our life.

ANTHONY: Why do you say that?

EVA: It is said that you are what you eat. But it is more accurate to say you are what you worship. Man does not live by bread alone. Since you are going to suffer and die as a result of living, in choosing to worship God, your death can be regarded as a fulfillment. Anything less than this is the worship of an idol.

ANTHONY: But we're vampires, we don't die.

EVA: Yes and what a cruel fate this is. To live forever and never experience God's grace. It's the case that most vampires die as a result of self-immolation, you know. The need for sacrifice is strong even among our ranks.

ANTHONY: I can't argue with you on this; I long to be human again. But I see great danger in abandonment of reason and the wholesale adoption of faith. That's how naïve people get exploited.

EVA: People of blind faith should be exploited; they are naïve and they think that God is some sort of benevolent Santa Claus that makes a list of who is naughty and who is nice. Rain falls on the good and the evil alike. The application of reason to faith is necessary for the spirit to progress. A process some Christian theologians refer to as sanctification. Reason alone yields hubris, faith alone piety. Reasonable faith requires courage to ask and humility to accept the answer. This is the purpose of prayer. Secular academics refer to this as a research question.

ANTHONY: I see your point. I know my fair share of prima donna academics. But why do you need faith in research?

EVA: The truth is hard to tolerate. We've created 'safe-spaces' so that students can live their own truth or simply avoid any reality they don't like. This a secular response to an existential problem: How do you handle the problem of existence with all the suffering to which flesh is heir?

ANTHONY: I agree with you about safe-spaces, students are far less tolerant these days. I hate having to preface practically everything that I say with a trigger warning. Truth is uncomfortable and if you say anything of any significance offending someone is inevitable. Although

I'm not sure how religion offers anything better.

EVA: Secularism invariably collapses under the weight of its own conceit. Reason deals with a certain class of problems well. It is just the rest of reality that is the problem.

ANTHONY: You'll have to explain that.

EVA: Both science and religion deal with the problem of a complex and ultimately unknowable universe. They just deal with it differently. They are not incompatible when it is understood their response to complexity is different. Scientism with its emphasis on reason and rationality will tend to frame the problem of complexity as one that is epistemologically uncertain. This theory of knowledge operates on the assumption that it is possible to specify the uncertainty in objective terms. This being the case, the research objective is to discover the outcome based on known facts and stated limitations. Religion, by contrast, accepts that we cannot objectively specify the nature of reality, existence and being. Complexity in religion is framed as a problem that is ontologically indeterminate. The future is inherently unknowable and faith enables us to step forward in the face of that indeterminacy. There is no way to control life and run the experiment again to empirically confirm the results. You have one life and no one knows what happens when we die. The only outcomes that are available to us are the ones we have imagined. Religion populates our imagination and faith moves us forward. What we believe affects how we behave and will in turn characterize the meaning of our lives. Life with all its latent potential cannot be subject to objective specification. Scientific reductionism has as its goal the grinding down of man to the molecular level, turning human beings into human resources. It's no accident that corporations have HR departments.

ANTHONY: I can't say I've thought of it this way. I've always thought of religious types as being mindless cult followers.

EVA: Some are, but by the same token you would not describe all academics as paragons of reason either. They are often the most petty, self-absorbed, neurotic people on the planet.

ANTHONY [laughs]: That would make a great job description!

EVA: It would. We shy away from these topics in the university. The other day I had to sit through a meeting debating whether we could have a Christmas tree in the common area. It was going to be called a festive tree in any event but the idea was shot down as reinforcing the dominant hegemony. It's a strange time when tolerance serves as a mask for totalitarianism.

ANTHONY: But don't you think the university should have the goal of realizing the potential of students and their personal development?

EVA: Students all have potential; they also all have limitations. We tend to dislike discomfort in our safe spaces. Understanding limitations and making decisions under hard constraints and limited information necessarily requires strength of character. Unfortunately, this quality is not developed with academic pillow fighting. Undergraduates have four years in which to develop themselves and define their purpose. However university administrations increasingly cater to the student experience; they leave like marshmallows ready to be roasted on the corporate campfire.

ANTHONY: That might be going a bit too far. There must be more to personal development than that. What about growth in personal autonomy and intellectual independence?

EVA: Personal development, self-love and living your truth are based on the individual's feelings. But feelings are transitory at best. Trying to make happiness last based on what feels right in the moment is like trying to catch the wind. It makes for a life that is both quixotic and chaotic. Have you heard of the law of mimetic desire?

ANTHONY: No.

EVA: The term was first introduced by the philosopher Rene Girard. Girard observed that man is the creature who does not know what to desire, and he turns to others in order to make up his mind. We desire what others desire because we imitate their desires — a mimesis. No one springs out of the womb knowing exactly what they want to do. We copy even though we do not understand. This process characterizes all human behavior. There is no escape from this, the only choice we have once we have developed sufficient cognitive ability, is who or what we choose to imitate. Faithful Christians attempt to imitate Christ — a life that cannot be duplicated but one that is everlasting. In this way, their lives give expression to their highest ideals.

ANTHONY: I think Jordan Peterson makes a similar point about taking responsibility and sacrifice for a noble goal.

EVA: Peterson gets a lot of things right. However, he makes the secularist error of applying reason to a space that should be occupied by faith. While he recognizes the Bible as the foundation for the manifestation of truth in Western society, he professes to act as if God exists. He is unwilling to submit to what he so clearly articulates is a higher authority. Since we have established that you are what you worship, it is possible to fall into the self-realization trap of fashioning an idol from one's own will rather than conforming to Christ.

ANTHONY: I've always wondered what that means, to worship an idol.

EVA: The concept of idolatry is very valuable. We can make an idol out of anything: Family, Career, Success, Wealth, Image, etc. It's really anything that takes the place of God in your heart. Calvin remarked that the human heart is a 'factory of idols.' Family, success, etc. are not inherently bad of course; Peterson makes the claim that if we improve our lives along these dimensions we will develop our character and strengthen our communities. But these things don't last. Trying to make these things permanent, we cause suffering and rob ourselves of joy. By seeking to hold onto it, to control it, we lose the thing we love. This I think is the meaning behind Jesus' statement, 'But seek ye first the kingdom of God, and his righteousness; and all these things shall be added unto you.'. We are required to align our desire with God's will, trusting that He works in our best interest in ways that are incomprehensible to us. At some point human reason must yield to faith and this occurs when Truth has entered into the human heart. I provide research support to a lot of highly intellectual people; the most dangerous are the ones that are also arrogant. Unbridled intellect can rationalize the most immoral actions. Similarly, blind faith is equally problematic because it can so easily be manipulated and exploited.

ANTHONY: That's deep. I'll have to think about this. What do you think this all means for the future of higher education?

EVA: Education takes its etymological root from the Latin *educare* meaning to lead out. If the university is to serve its pedagogical function it must necessarily be leading to something higher. Academic freedom comes with responsibility. Ultimately faith must be the foundation of intellectual community otherwise our research agendas will be controlled by the university administration and besieged by market forces. Increasingly sophisticated efforts will be made to empirically validate the performance of academics in the first instance and more broadly to the knowledge workers in the information economy in the second. Human relationships will become more transactional and commodified as students become increasingly treated as consumers of education rather than seekers of truth. The absence of a higher ideal on which to aim one's life will result in correlative loss of meaning. This in turn will breed mental illnesses such as depression and anxiety. In order to not lose revenue and not be perceived as a toxic environment, the university will allow more and more student accommodations, creating activist students protesting for more rights and accepting less respon-sibility. They will become more bitter and angry and less tolerant of others as they get older, but by then it will be too late to do anything about it.

ANTHONY: So what happens in the end?

EVA: Students and their professors that turn away from God will become lifeless, soulless and always seeking blood.

ANTHONY: You mean like us?

EVA: Exactly like us, only mortal.

The Abortion

Over the last two months Anthony has been having an affair with his graduate student, Jessica Khan. Jessica is a promising Ph.D. candidate under Anthony's direct supervision. Anthony transgresses the cardinal rule of the vampire academic: Never have sex with a student. The affair ends as quickly as it began. Anthony confesses his affair to Ursula after Jessica tells him that she is pregnant. With only two months before her scheduled dissertation defense, Jessica has an abortion. Anthony takes her to the abortion clinic for the procedure and has her stay overnight at the home he shares with Ursula. While Jessica is recovering from the procedure, Anthony and Ursula discuss the events of the day.

URSULA: So how did it go?

ANTHONY: How do you think?

URSULA: So what happened?

ANTHONY: Well we turned up to the clinic and they explained everything to us. It was all matter-of-fact, really. Everyone in the waiting room sat silently, avoiding eye contact and afraid. They looked so pale in there, they could almost be mistaken for vampires.

URSULA: Stop being so dramatic. Were the staff any good?

ANTHONY: As you would expect. The nurse went over the procedure beforehand and gave Jess the disclaimer form at the end. What I thought was funny was how there was nowhere for me to sign.

URSULA: Why would there be?

ANTHONY: It was my baby, too.

URSULA: Are you fucking kidding me?! Your baby? You had nothing to do with it. It wasn't a baby, it was just a clump of cells. She wouldn't be in that mess if you had kept it in your pants. You don't get to have an opinion on this. How could you do that to her? To me?

ANTHONY: I'm sorry for that. For everything. For hurting you especially. I was wrong and I'm sorry. I should never have allowed myself to become involved. Pregnancy tissue is what they called it — the abortion clinic. I can admit that I'm wrong, but saying it's just a clump of cells isn't accurate, it's dehumanizing. Human beings are more than just clumps of cells at different stages of development.

URSULA: You really are a complete asshole, Anthony. You don't get to take the moral high ground here. You've been talking to Eva, haven't you? That sanctimonious bitch. What you are calling a baby would have most likely killed her. Not to mention completely wrecked her career.

ANTHONY: I'm sure the fetus didn't see it that way.

URSULA: Fetus? There you go again! It was nothing at that stage of gestation.

ANTHONY: OK then, at what stage does it become something?

URSULA: You know the rules, when it's viable outside the womb and can survive on its own.

ANTHONY: I know the rules, but that doesn't mean I agree; they don't make sense. It's not as if any human being is born and is instantly able to fend for themselves. Humans are an interdependent species. Who gets to decide who lives and who dies? Plus viability varies with advances in medical technology. More and more babies survive after being born prematurely every year.

URSULA: Lines have to be drawn and we have decided that as a society, you're free to think what you like. Anyway what you're saying is irrelevant. It was her body, it was her choice. Plus it's not like it could feel or think or have any of the attributes that make up a human being.

ANTHONY: My body, my choice is a protest poster, it's not an argument. Your reasoning doesn't make sense. You're basing viability on what a woman wants. If she wants to be pregnant, what's inside her is a baby, if she doesn't then it's nothing worth caring about.

URSULA: The woman was here first. It is her right to choose, not the government's and certainly not yours.

ANTHONY: So who lives and who dies depends on what women want? God help us all.

URSULA: Fuck God. God has nothing to do with this.

ANTHONY: God has everything to do with this. Conception of life is either something or it is nothing. If God doesn't exist, there is no good, no evil, right or wrong. We don't need to have this conversation since it doesn't matter. One idea or action is as good (or bad) as another. Human beings are nothing more than random organic matter acting upon chance. Without a fixed reference point – God – There is nothing to judge good or bad. You can define your own reality and live your own 'Truth.'

URSULA: I wouldn't go that far. You talk of morality, like you're in charge of it. Making a woman have a child she doesn't want is immoral. Why bring a child into this world that you don't want or can't take care of? Jessica has the rest of her life to live. You know how difficult it is to get a tenure track position, much less secure tenure. How is she expected to do that without help? Where would she have gotten that from, you? You created this problem.

ANTHONY: I'm pretty sure that babies don't give a shit about Google Scholar citations or whether or not she gets tenure. Your whole line of argument is based on it being her body and her choice. But that is not entirely accurate either.

URSULA: How do you figure that?

ANTHONY: A fetus isn't a woman's body, it's *inside* her body. A woman's uterus is in her body but it is designed for no other purpose than to carry a baby. A fact she is reminded of each month. If that's correct, then the fetus has a right to access its mother's womb in order to live for nine months.

URSULA: That's ridiculous. You're essentially arguing for forced pregnancy. Women are not just walking wombs. They have goals and dreams too. They deserve the freedom to choose.

ANTHONY: Forced pregnancy? It's not like I raped her. That would be a crime. We don't call being prohibited from killing your toddler forced parenting. Society has no problem forcing men to support children they have fathered once paternity has been established.

URSULA: That's because it's the right thing to do.

ANTHONY: I don't disagree. But then you're OK with women having the option of terminating their own child just because it cannot at that moment survive without them. How long do you think women would survive without men?

URSULA: Women have always been burdened with having children. Giving them control over their reproductive choices has levelled the playing field. It has allowed them to participate in the economy in ways that were previously unimaginable.

ANTHONY: Well men have always been burdened with putting their lives at risk for women and children. You seem to take that fact for granted. What's worse is they are still expected to do that. Women want equality, but only when it suits them. Modern technologies such as the internet have created a burgeoning service sector. A knowledge economy. This has allowed women to participate in high-paying white-collar jobs. But the internet relies on the telecommunications infrastructure, which was built and is maintained for the most part by men. When the electricity goes out, you don't see feminists scaling hydro poles attempting to restore power. We take these things for granted, because we take men for granted. They're expendable. This has always been the case. What's different is that we have come to believe that the unborn are expendable too.

URSULA: So you're saying that women should just make babies and live a life of domestic slavery like it's the 1950s?

ANTHONY: No Ursula, I'm not saying that at all. Women have more choices than they have ever had at any point in history. They are also more miserable and lonelier than ever. When exactly did the aspiration to be a wife and a mother become a bad life choice? A burden. What's unfair is that young women are lied to that they can have a career and contribute to a family without compromise. That's simply untrue. Modern women regard a man's life as an al-a-carte menu, they can simply pick and choose which parts they want. They complain that they are not getting into C-suite positions in blue chip companies, they don't complain about the fact that most of the shitty jobs that still have to be done are positions that are primarily occupied by men.

URSULA: I never said that being a housewife is a bad choice, women should have the option to do that too.

ANTHONY: You seem to think that biological imperatives are optional, but they are not. Men and women are biologically different, that is a fact. If a woman wants to act like a man, she should not be surprised when she is treated like one and vice versa. Your theory is that giving women control over their own bodies would result in greater equality for all. But that hasn't happened. Abortion is a moral wrong, no amount of self-serving rationalization can result in the inescapable moral consequences of that decision. You seem to reduce abortion to the moral equivalent of a tooth extraction, but if I had taken Jessica to the dentist this morning we wouldn't be having this conversation.

URSULA: So what about rape or incest? Do you think women should not be allowed to have an abortion under those circumstances?

ANTHONY: Well that's a bit extreme since rape and incest account for a small fraction of pregnancies in the first place; the vast majority of abortions are elective. Rape and incest are moral wrongs, there's no question about that. But does it follow that terminating an unborn child is morally right?

URSULA: But why should a girl that's been raped have to suffer the consequences of some man's decision to violate her?

ANTHONY: There's no question that terminating the pregnancy makes the most sense. Who could not understand that having a lifetime reminder of being raped would be traumatic? We can agree that the rapist is guilty and should be punished, but can we also agree that the unborn child is innocent and should not be punished.

URSULA: So you would make her have the baby, you selfish prick!

ANTHONY: I wouldn't force her to be a parent to that baby. She could put the baby up for adoption. That is an option.

URSULA: That's a very convenient position to take for someone who's never given birth.

ANTHONY: What is convenient is the taking of an innocent life because it does not happen to fall into your personal plans. Having sex comes with a risk of having an unwanted pregnancy. While we have significantly reduced that risk through reliable birth control, that risk is not zero. But just because the pregnancy is unwanted, it doesn't follow that the unborn child can be deemed pregnancy tissue and discarded like a Kleenex.

URSULA: You must be very happy that Roe v. Wade got overturned.

ANTHONY: As a matter of legal reasoning, I thought it made sense. Whether you agree with abortion laws or not is ultimately a political question that should be decided by the legislature and not the judiciary. I never quite understood how constitutionally protected freedoms of liberty and privacy could be interpreted to enshrine a woman's right to terminate her child.

URSULA: Well, in free and democratic societies privacy is interpreted as the freedom to make intimate and personal choices that are central to personal dignity and autonomy.

ANTHONY: That all sounds nice until you realize that you are in effect engaged in state-sanctioned murder.

URSULA: Almost no one but those evangelical lunatics seriously thinks that.

ANTHONY: People have the right to their opinions. Calling them lunatics is not a principled basis on which to reject their argument.

URSULA: I just don't think it's right. If you ban abortions, women will just find other more dangerous methods of achieving the same ends. Do you really want to go back to using coat hangers in back alleys?

ANTHONY: Now look who is being dramatic. It's something of human nature to want pleasure without pain. If anyone does not understand that the act of sexual intercourse carries with it the possibility of having a child, that person is either stupid or naïve. You don't just get to say, 'I made a mistake, I want a do-over.'

URSULA: So you're saying that we should all be virgins until marriage and then be platonic 'till death do us part' so we don't ever get a child we don't want?

ANTHONY: Look, I'm not perfect and I don't claim to have all the answers. But I do think that we should acknowledge right from wrong, even when we're on the wrong side of the line — especially when we're on the wrong side of the line. The road Roe led us down was paved with good intentions, but it has resulted in millions of innocent lives terminated. Fewer marriages, more divorces, an epidemic of mental illness and loneliness. In the absence of responsibility, more choice tends to create more chaos. That's not progress, that's social degeneration.

URSULA: You're wrong. What's the point of bringing a child into this world that no one wants?

ANTHONY: You should be specific here. You mean what's the point of bringing a child into this world that the mother doesn't want.

URSULA: Fair enough. It's her life that will be most affected. It's her body that's going to get ruined by the pregnancy, it's her career that's going down the toilet. And for what? So she can be shackled to a baby and dependent on a man for the rest of her life? It's her life too, doesn't her choice matter too?

ANTHONY: It does. But, as we have discussed, for the most part women make a choice to have sex with a man. That choice always has a risk of pregnancy attached to it. In the rare instances that she has had sex without consent, she still has a responsibility to not harm the innocent life that is inside her. Why should women not be held accountable for their choices?

URSULA: The bottom line is if a woman wants an abortion she should get an abortion.

ANTHONY: When?

URSULA: What do you mean? Whenever she wants one!

ANTHONY: At what point during the gestational period should abortion be permitted?

URSULA: I don't know, 12 weeks. Maybe more depending on the circumstances.

ANTHONY: So she should be required to have the baby after 12 weeks?

URSULA: I guess. If she can't get it together after 3 months then that's on her.

ANTHONY: So for you, women have 3 months grace period to decide whether or not the life inside them will be allowed to be born?

URSULA: Yes. Sure.

ANTHONY: So the youngest premature baby to survive is around 21 weeks. Advances in neonatal care are likely to reduce this time even further. What is the reasoning for elective abortion at any point during the first 12 weeks?

URSULA: Accidents happen. People need second chances.

ANTHONY: Pregnancy isn't an accident, it is a consequence. You think women should have second chances, but not men.

URSULA: I didn't say that.

ANTHONY: You didn't have to.

URSULA: Lower your voice, she's waking up.

ANTHONY: Let's see if she needs anything.

Student Life

The Seculari are a clandestine group of tenured vampire academics. Among other things they evaluate the performance of other vampire academics and determine whether they should be granted tenure for eternity. Although Anthony's academic performance has been good, he has little hope of obtaining tenure with the scandal he has been involved in. Several months have passed since the Seculari have passed judgment upon Anthony. Vampire academics that do not make tenure perish in a very real sense as they are put to death. Anthony's death has been made to look like a suicide so as not to arouse suspicion. A group of his students meet at a bar on campus to discuss the impact that Anthony had on their lives and his intellectual legacy.

NANCY: I can't believe he took his own life. Something very Jeffrey Epstein about it all.

GREG: Except he wasn't a pedophile, in jail or super rich.

NANCY: But you know what I mean. He just doesn't seem the type that would do something like that.

SAM: Yeah, you never really know what's going on in someone's life. Lots of people can look perfectly fine on the outside and yet mask pain that runs really deep.

NANCY: But somehow the facts just don't add up. I mean he was a great prof, well respected at the university. I blew off so many classes, but I had to attend his class. He was so engaging and provocative.

GREG: Provocative?

NANCY: I mean, I was offended by a lot of what he had to say about women at the time. But I think differently now and it's because of him. Do you remember his story about Perseus and Andromeda?

SAM: And how we'd all be doomed if we embraced androgyny?

NANCY: Yeah.

GREG: I wasn't there for that class.

NANCY: He argued that Perseus and Andromeda is an archetypal myth on the roles of men and women. He said that the story revealed far more truth and meaning than all the feminist diatribes combined.

GREG: How do you figure that?

NANCY: The myth of Perseus and Andromeda has been with us for millennia. It's inspired art and literature throughout the centuries.

SAM: Yes. He said in class that in comparison, feminism has been with us all of five seconds. What got me was how he related the fundamental storyline of the hero, Perseus, rescuing Andromeda, the damsel in distress. When he compared that to Super Mario Bros. I just lost it! You don't understand it when you're a kid, you just play the game. I didn't understand it even as an adult. The idea is that Mario has to go through all his challenges and finally defeat the big boss, Bowser, in order to save Princess Peach. You think you're just playing a game. But it defines the course of your life because it brings focus to action. You perceive it to be important, but you don't know why. It enables you to act in the face of uncertainty. Without this fundamental orientation, our lives lack meaning. So much of today's discourse is about 'living your truth,' which he used to say was nonsense.

NANCY: Yes. But feminists complained that the damsel in distress is a trope used to oppress women in patriarchal societies. According to them, women can be independent and don't need rescuing. They can do it on their own. For centuries men and women have cooperated with each other to face life with all its trials and tribulations together, drawing on each other's strengths. Feminism swept away history and biology and pitted the sexes against each other.

SAM: Kevin Samuels makes a similar point in the black community where the problems are more pronounced. Black women have advanced themselves in the workplace and been fooled into believing material and career success would make them better marital prospects, but the men they tend to attract are generally weak and effeminate. Beta males, as Samuels puts it. Although a relationship with such a person might look good on Instagram, it is rotten to the core. A woman will find it hard to love a man she does not respect. She won't trust him, because she knows if she can control him, others can too. Perseus by contrast is The Man. He has the masculine essence and has acquired skills along his journey. Those experiences have made him valuable. Women want him and men want to be him. He asks her parents to marry her and doesn't ask Andromeda if she wants to be rescued. That can be assumed. He's not on Tinder and he doesn't have to slide into a hot girl's DMs.

GREG: And what about Andromeda? Isn't she just reduced to a sex object – a trophy?

SAM: I used to think that. I used to think that it was so unfair, that men got to have the adventures and their fun and women had to just sit there waiting around to be picked. Invariably they end up choosing assholes. But then, relationships are reflective. We tend to get what we are. When you think about it, Andromeda is the focus of the story. She's Perseus' mirror. Without her, there is no story. She is the reason that Perseus is prepared to risk life and limb. Andromeda is no ordinary girl. She is the paragon of femininity. As a virgin she offers Perseus the prospect of leaving a legacy and an opportunity to go where no man has gone before.

GREG: Ha!

SAM: An important element of the story is the fact that the reason Andromeda is in chains is due to the fact that her mother bragged about her beauty and offended the gods.

GREG: Why is that important?

SAM: Women are often oppressed and sometimes the cultural traditions favour some more than others. But that's true for both men, women and different racial groups, etc. But in most societies, Western societies in particular, it is women that oppress other women. Have you ever watched an episode of *The Real Housewives*?

GREG: Which one? There are so many!

SAM: Exactly! The show is that popular. The *Real Housewives* shows are in high demand and they primarily cater to a female audience. Every single Housewife show is about women engaged in conspicuous consumption and character assassination. Women as a TV demographic love watching *The Real Housewives* for the same reason that I love MMA. We love to fight.

NANCY: I'm not sure I follow you. How is mixed martial arts the same as *The Real Housewives*?

SAM: They're not. It's just that men fight with their hands and women fight with their mouths.

NANCY: Excuse me?

SAM: OK maybe that's not the best way of putting it. But you have to admit that women fight differently to men. *The Real Housewives* is a masterclass on how women backbite, gossip and gang up on each other in order to damage another girl's reputation or socially exclude her from the group.

GREG: Yeah, I don't get where you're going with this; there is a referee in MMA.

SAM: Yes! Not only is there a referee in the ring determining whether everyone fights fair. You don't get to bring a weapon or put lead in your gloves in a boxing match. There is also a weigh-in before the bout. You never see a title fight between a heavyweight and a featherweight. Weight classes exist for a reason.

GREG: OK.

SAM: Well when you have controlled for all the factors that would otherwise make the fight unfair you are able to let the best man win. That's equality. As a collective, women say they want equality, but as individuals what women want is she-quality! The rules have to be set up so she can win every single time, but everyone should act like the fight was fair!

GREG: That's crazy!

SAM: Not crazy. Female logic. Modern women hate being made accountable for their bad behavior.

GREG: You're going to have to give an example for that.

SAM: Where to start? Look at all the campaigns we have on sexual assault. You would think that women are getting raped as soon as they step onto campus. We blindly adopt the mantra 'Believe women' as if there was no need for the rule of law or the idea of being innocent until proven guilty. On the way in here I saw a marketing campaign on consent being as easy as FRIES.

NANCY: FRIES?

SAM: Consent is Freely Given, Reversible, Informed, Enthusiastic, and Specific. FRIES. Here, I'll bring it up on my phone. Consent is an active, direct, voluntary, unimpaired and conscious choice and agreement to engage or continue in sexual activity. Consent to one act does not mean consent to another. It goes on to say that consent is never assumed or implied, is not silence or the absence of 'no,' etc., etc.

NANCY: Yeah that's a bit much.

SAM: A bit much. It's practically impossible to ask a girl out anymore without her thinking you're a serial rapist! We're set up to fail. What a woman feels seems to be the only truth that matters. If she feels like you're 'the one,' then the FRIES can go out the window. If she doesn't, you'd better have your legal team assembled because she's coming for your shit. That's why the Red Pill, MGTOW movement has gained so much traction. Men are sick of getting screwed over.

NANCY: But you have to admit men are more likely to harm women physically in domestic disputes.

SAM: Maybe. But then women initiate most of the fights. They do this with verbal taunts, insults, etc. It's their way of fighting.

NANCY: Come on.

SAM: You know it's true. Women have been made so safe in our society, they think they can say whatever they want without consequence. And you know what, until the system crashes down they're right. Men don't have that luxury. I can't say whatever I want to Greg without things escalating into physical confrontation eventually. The threat of violence keeps things civilized.

NANCY: That's not true. I feel vulnerable all the time, especially at night.

SAM: But the difference is that you always have the option of playing the little woman and you know there will be another man to come to your rescue. Look at Ukraine. They conscripted every able-bodied man aged 18-60 to stay and fight the Russian invasion. Suddenly every woman is a traditional housewife that loves kids. There's not a 'me too' hashtag in sight!

NANCY: Well, gender stereotypes do exist for a reason.

SAM: Of course you would say that. What about equality? That's why I say that women only want equality when it suits them. That's why you would be an idiot to get married as a man these days. Marriage holds nothing for a man other than granting his wife the legal right to half his stuff and all the kids they had together. A man's physical strength can be abused, that's for sure. But a man's ability to coerce by force is limited in a myriad of ways by our institutions and other men. What is not so clear is how female power, which lies in their physical beauty and their ability to manipulate men emotionally, can be constrained. Modern women want all the benefits of the tradition, but none of the obligations that go with it. Men by contrast are expected to be responsible for everything but with zero authority to make decisions relating to their own families. Women are OK with being traditional if it feels right to them. But feelings are beside the point.

NANCY: What was that MGTOW you were going on about before?

GREG: It stands for Men Going Their Own Way. It's a group of loser guys that opted out of relationships with women. They call it the red pill, a reference to *The Matrix* where Morpheus gives Neo the option to see reality for what it is or take the blue pill and remain plugged into a system that will rob him of his free will. I think it's just sad.

SAM: Not sad. It's a rational response to the current reality. Women's expectations in relationships are unrealistic because they think they can 'let it go' like Elsa in the movie *Frozen*. They can be strong and independent and find true love like Anna. But life is not a fucking Disney movie. Men, being the idiots that we are, go along with this crap until the whole thing crashes down. Women rarely call each other out on their bad behavior. We're socially conditioned like Pavlov's dogs to BELIEVE WOMEN when women are the biggest liars ever.

GREG: That's not true.

SAM: Stop trying to get in Nancy's pants, Greg. She's not going to get with you if you just keep agreeing with her and even if she does, the sex will suck and she'll dump you eventually.

GREG: You're an asshole.

SAM: Keep your pants on, G-Man. I'm just kidding. Anyway, what was I saying? Ah yes. Look at the stats. 1 in 10 dads are not the biological father of their child. Men get suckered into taking care of kids that are not their own all the time. This problem could easily be solved by making paternity tests mandatory at birth. But would this ever happen? Hell would have to freeze over before that ever happened. Why? This would make women actually responsible for their reproductive choices. They would have to wake up from their Disney delusions.

NANCY: There are other reasons too. Many bio fathers wouldn't make good dads. I'm mean, the girl chose the guy she's with to be her child's father for a reason. He should be happy with that. Besides, where's the love and trust in the relationship?

SAM: Are you listening to yourself? You would be OK with having a random chump take care of a kid that wasn't his own just because the girl felt he was the father?

NANCY: No, she's just doing the best for herself and her kid. So what if he's not the father; everyone, including the kid, will treat him as such. What else is she going to do?

SAM: How about telling the truth! How about taking responsibility for her actions and not screwing another man's life over? This is the problem — few women, save some brave souls like Janice Fiamingo, speak out on these issues.

NANCY: Women get screwed over all the time.

GREG: I have to admit that's kind of messed up.

SAM: These are problems only women — sane women, not feminists — can solve. It's like the problem of transgenderism. The rainbow flag wasn't good enough so they kept on adding colours and letters until we can't define what a woman is anymore.

NANCY: Yeah, I draw the line at the bathroom.

SAM: A line has to be drawn somewhere, otherwise we're living in a world without boundaries and this is just chaos. Perhaps that's the point. Maybe we want to live in a world of birthing people and chest feeders so that the MAPs can have free reign.

GREG: What are MAPs?

SAM: Minor-attracted persons, otherwise known as pedophiles. You probably wondered what the plus sign meant in LGBTQ2+

GREG: I think Dave Chappelle calls them the alphabet people.

SAM: I never understood what was wrong with just saying gay and straight.

NANCY: It's not inclusive.

SAM: It's nonsensical, is what it is.

NANCY: Are you serious about the MAPs thing?

SAM: The fact that you have to ask that just shows how wrong things have become. We never say anything or anyone is wrong anymore. No one stands their ground because they have no idea where the line is drawn.

GREG: Anyway, did you ever know what happened to Jessica Khan?

NANCY: I saw her speak at a Women in STEM conference recently. She was talking about the challenges of obtaining tenure with trying to start a family. She said that she's freezing her eggs until she meets the right person.

SAM: Wasn't she with Prof. M?

NANCY: That's the rumour. I heard he broke it off with her before she graduated.

GREG: I checked out her Insta recently, she has a lot of cats.

SAM: There's a study that women without kids get cats because their meows sound like babies.

NANCY: You're full of it!

SAM: Egg freezing is just another way of women extending their Disney princess syndrome into their mid-forties.

NANCY: What do you mean?

SAM: Take Jessica as an example. She could have married someone in her 20s and had kids. But no, she chose to ignore her biological clock and now she's expecting her employer to pay for fertility treatments. Why should my tuition money be spent on saving Jessica Khan from the consequences of her poor life choices?

GREG: It's not as simple as that.

SAM: Stop simping, Greg. It's not rocket science. Jessica wanted it all on her own terms. She mistakenly thought she could pursue her career and there would be a man that would sweep her off her feet and they would have 2.5 kids and live happily ever after. Now she's bitter because the man she wants to be with doesn't want her.

NANCY: Why not? I think she's amazing.

SAM: Of course you would say that, and I dare say if you were a lesbian she'd be your cup of tea. But most men don't care for women with PhDs. It doesn't make you hotter to us.

NANCY: That's because you're shallow and aren't able to handle a strong and independent woman.

SAM: No, I value my peace and sanity. Men naturally want to provide for and protect women and children. You see this in any crisis. It's always women and children first. Look at the death stats of the Titanic. It was men that went down with the ship. If there are a limited number of lifeboats, you better believe that men will get them last. Men don't ask for much other than being appreciated for the sacrifices they are required to make. Women complain that men aren't 'stepping up' but they never realize how shitty life is for the ordinary man. Regular dudes are pretty much invisible to most women. Women get all the attention when they're young. If they're unmarried and in their 40s they get to experience what most men in their 20s experience every day. Not being noticed, having to deal with getting rejected all the time. Jessica has fallen into this trap. She thought she could have fun in her 20s, pursue her career and land a man who would be her equal or higher. But that limits her mate selection to assistant or tenured profs, and guess what? Most of those guys are married. Her competition for that man isn't women with PhDs, it's hot grads in their late 20s.

GREG: I think Jessica has still got it. Have you seen her profile pic?

SAM: Get some standards, dumbass!

GREG: [Laughs]

SAM: Egg freezing is a prime example of what Prof. M. termed technological millennialism — the belief that technology would solve everything including the problem it creates. He argued that with the decline of religion, technology would become its own religion, because human beings need something to worship. It's just a question of what they worship and with what consequence. The worship of technology, he said, explains how human beings became human resources. We believe what we feel is real. Gender has become a personal feeling rather than a biological fact. We can make and unmake ourselves according to how we feel, because that is all that we value. We think we're being authentic, but we're actually being neurotic. Ultimately the scientific rationalizations animate the secularist agenda and result in human reason getting sacrificed on the altar of technological efficiency. We create the machines and then become slaves to them. We no longer are reasonable because we are unable to reason. Smart tech has made us dumb. All that matters is that we conform to the current ideology until we are no longer able to think for ourselves.

GREG: I was there for that class. Prof. M compared artificial intelligence to the Tower of Babel. In man's quest to grasp the transcendent, he loses purpose and meaning. It's a powerful metaphor. Human nature strives to build itself to rival God only to be defeated time and time again, until we ask, do you serve your religion or does your religion serve you?

SAM: Yes, and by extension we assume incorrectly that the teleological end of law and policy is to maximize choice. This rests on the false belief that man is rational and will optimize the system via his self-interest. Man cannot know his interest apart from God. Law and policy are, fundamentally, expressions of morality that either arcs toward the creator or away from him.

GREG: Hold that thought, I'm just going to the washroom. [Leaves]

NANCY: So I've been having trouble putting this IKEA furniture together. You worked at IKEA didn't you?

SAM: Yes...

NANCY: So you know how to put up shelving units, right?

SAM: Yes...

NANCY: So do you still have the skills?

SAM: Yes...I see where you're going with this, I just want you to ask.

NANCY: Do you want to come over and help me?

SAM: What's in it for me?

NANCY: I don't know, what?

SAM: OK, text me your address.

GREG [Returns]: Hey, I have to get going. I have an interview with Prof. Ursula.

SAM: Oh yeah. What are you interviewing for?

GREG: She's looking for a TA.

SAM: That's cool. Good luck man.

GREG: Do you guys wanna hang out later?

NANCY: Thanks, but it's been a long day and I'm just going to go home and relax.

SAM: Yeah, I've got a bunch of stuff to do, so...

GREG: No problem. Catch up with you later.

SAM: Take it easy.

NANCY: Bye.

Trial Prep

Nancy and Sam have sex after meeting at the bar. When confronted by her boyfriend Mike, Nancy falsely accuses Sam of rape. Mike believes and supports Nancy. He insists that she go to the police. Nancy reluctantly agrees. The police believe that there is sufficient evidence to arrest and charge Sam. Sam is currently a law student studying for the bar exams. He retains Grant McKenna as his criminal defense lawyer. In this dialogue, Sam and his lawyer prepare for trial and discuss the issues surrounding his case.

GRANT: How are you holding up?

SAM: To be honest, not well. This has been hell. I feel like my life has been turned upside down.

GRANT: That's to be expected. Just know I'm here to help and if there's anything you need, just let me know.

SAM: Thanks, I appreciate that.

GRANT: I've reviewed your file and as you know the charges are pretty serious. The good news is that the evidence against you is pretty thin. Just so I know I haven't missed anything, why don't you tell me in your own words what happened.

SAM: So the three of us...

GRANT: Three?

SAM: Yeah, myself, Nancy and a mutual friend Greg.

GRANT: Did Greg see you go home with Nancy?

SAM: No, he left earlier.

GRANT: But you were all drinking together?

SAM: Right.

GRANT: OK. Please continue

SAM: We arrived at Nancy's place. Her boyfriend wasn't home. She invited me up to set up her IKEA furniture. When she got there, we had another drink. We were both pretty drunk by that point since we'd already been drinking at the bar. We were on the couch and she started lightly stroking the inside of my thigh. We kissed, moved to the bedroom and did it there. Although we were both drunk it was totally consensual.

GRANT: Did you use a condom?

SAM: She said not to worry about it. She's on the pill. I didn't have any on me and when I asked her she joked that Mike's condoms would be too small for me.

GRANT: Hmm. OK. We'll have to work with that. You need to be aware that she paints a very different story. According to her you were asked up to help her with her IKEA furniture. She passed out on the couch fully clothed. When she woke up she was naked and had been raped.

SAM: That's a fucking lie!

GRANT: Listen, if we're going to get through this you're going to have to remain calm. I'm on your side. But the prosecutor is not.

SAM: Sorry, I just don't know what I'm going to do. If I get a conviction for sexual assault, they'll never let me practice law. I have so much student debt as it is. My parents have re-mortgaged their house at this point. All because of one stupid night.

GRANT: I completely understand why you're upset. Just try to think of the next step. Which at this point is trying to get the prosecutor to drop the charges against you.

SAM: So you think that's a possibility? I thought you said the prosecutor is not on my side.

GRANT: Well the prosecutor is not there to take sides. There's a saying that the Crown never wins and never loses. It means they're not supposed to care whether they convict, but rather to see justice is done. Now the reality is quite different of course. The prosecutor in this case is known for her activism.

SAM: What do you mean?

GRANT: She's made public statements about the number of women that tell her that the trial process felt worse than the rape. She wants to secure a conviction for the victims, which is fair enough, she has a job to do. The problem comes when we throw out the presumption of innocence.

SAM: Yeah, I used to believe in innocent until proven guilty until I got charged. Now even people in my own family look at me with suspicion. I somehow feel that even if I'm acquitted things will never be the same.

GRANT: You're not wrong. Things won't be the same after this.

SAM: But it would help if I knew how we got here, you know. I know that I'm innocent. So does Nancy. Doesn't that count for something? Shouldn't that matter?

GRANT: It should and it does. But we live in an increasingly politicized world — one where feelings have come to matter more than right and wrong, or perhaps more accurately, what is felt is regarded as the objective truth. Logic and reason are dispensed with when feelings and emotions take centre stage. It's for this reason that so many nitwits talk about my truth, or my lived experience, as if that should count in determining who is at fault. The legal system has been all but captured by the feminist narrative at this point.

SAM: Totally, I hate feminism! It's brought nothing but chaos in our society. It doesn't matter how much men do, it will never be enough. I'm so sick of that shit. You're so right. We are taught from a young age that mother knows best and to believe women. But what happens when they lie? We're supposed to turn a blind eye to their shitty behavior and have our faults highlighted every minute of every day. It's fucked up.

GRANT: Again, it's OK that you rant like that to me. This, unlike your university classroom, truly is a safe space, as our communications are subject to privilege. Remember always that I'm your lawyer and I represent you. Just don't advocate for violence against anyone; I'm required to report that.

SAM: OK. Nancy is lying; how come no one sees this?

GRANT: I'm afraid this is a consequence of the 'believe women' mantra that is so prevalent in our society today. It puts all the responsibility on men to fix things. Women can retain authority but never be at fault or held accountable.

SAM: I read a YouTube comment that said that women want the power and authority of a man, the privilege of being a woman, the account-ability of a child and the self-awareness of a fetus.

GRANT: That's some serious Red Pill you've taken, I'd caution you not to go too far down that particular rabbit hole. You're going to have to dial this down if we are to have any hope of getting through this. But I have to admit that you're not entirely wrong here. I've seen this in my own practice. There's a complete double-standard when it comes to assault for example.

SAM: Oh yeah?

GRANT: Sure. Women want equality, except when it comes to sentencing. Once convicted I've seen women that have committed heinous crimes transform themselves into harmless angels as they plead for a reduced sentence, which they consistently obtain. You are far more likely to get jail time as a man than a woman would for the same crime. No feminist cares about this fact.

SAM: It's so unfair. Women are plain evil.

GRANT: Some women are, some women will always be. There's a long history of female evil in Western Civilization that can be traced right back to the book of Genesis.

SAM: You mean Adam and Eve?

GRANT: Yes. It's as relevant today as it was when it first entered the collective consciousness of humanity.

SAM: Wasn't Eve basically evil?

GRANT: Not exactly, she was tempted by the serpent to eat the forbidden fruit, but Adam was derelict in his duty to protect Eve, so the deception took place on his watch, so to speak. When you think about it, the same has occurred in your case.

SAM: How do you figure that?

GRANT: Let's take a deeper look at the circumstances that have led you to be sitting in front of me charged with sexual assault. You knew that Nancy had a boyfriend, right?

SAM: Yeah, but...

GRANT: You were also alone with her and drinking, correct?

SAM: Yeah.

GRANT: You wanted her and she wanted you, yes?

SAM: Yes.

GRANT: Then why were you drinking?

SAM: I don't know, I guess because we were having fun and one thing led to another.

GRANT: Well I'm pretty sure it wasn't fun for Nancy's boyfriend.

SAM: Yeah, but what's he got to do with it?

GRANT: For the sexual assault, nothing. But then there's an ocean of difference between ethics and law, between sin and crime. I like to alert my clients to the moral dimensions of their situation. This helps them better process the verdict, whether guilty or innocent. While I'm only dealing with your criminal charges, there are a number of things that happened before you end up sitting in the chair in front of a criminal defense lawyer. There are important lessons for you to learn here, Sam.

Don't turn away from them. You have to break the pattern. But first you have to identify it.

SAM: I'm not sure what you mean.

GRANT: You need to accept responsibility for your role in precipitating this situation. By taking responsibility you will take back control of your life.

SAM: I still don't get it. Aren't you supposed to be my lawyer?

GRANT: Yes, but law is just the thin edge of a much larger ethical wedge. There are massive moral and ethical issues lurking underneath. These issues are not relevant for the criminal trial. In that forum we are only discussing the facts established by the admitted evidences and whether the elements of the crime of sexual assault have been established beyond reasonable doubt. But it's important to examine the ethical issues as they hold the key to deeper lessons that need to be learned if you have any hope of moving past this. Trust me, an ounce of ethical analysis will save you a ton of therapy; it will take you years to work through the anger, bitterness and resentment you will undoubtedly experience, if you don't deal with it now. Did you ever sleep with Nancy before or was this the first time?

SAM: First time.

GRANT: You see, casual sex is never casual. It's the thing no one tells you when you hook up with someone.

SAM: No, they don't.

GRANT: Have you ever thought of why that is?

SAM: Not really.

GRANT: Here's your first problem. Pretty much since the sixties there has been a relentless effort to decouple sex from commitment. Divorce rates have skyrocketed in that time. Far from being liberating it turns out that the sexual revolution was like sugar for relationships between the sexes, sweet to the taste but morally corrosive. Dating apps and porn have commodified human intimacy and produced a generation of miserable women and feeble men.

SAM: But I thought we're supposed to be equal. And didn't Pierre Trudeau famously say that, 'There is no place for the state in the bedrooms of the nation.'

GRANT: I'm afraid you are finding out the hard way that men and women are not equal. They never have been, they never will be. Especially when it comes to sex. It used to be the case that people waited until marriage to have sex. In the absence of reliable birth control this was really the only way to have sex. It's hard to underestimate just how much changed with The Pill.

SAM: But I don't understand. I wanted it, so did she, what's the problem?

GRANT: Just because you both wanted something and it felt good in the moment doesn't make it right, Sam. In former times you had to get married in order to have sex. People married much younger and had fewer sexual partners as a result. The consequences of engaging in premarital sex carried serious social repercussions. The language used to describe moral departure was different back then too. Adultery, for example, was used when at least one of the parties involved (either male or female) was married, whereas fornication described two people who are unmarried (to each other or anyone else) engaging in consensual sexual intercourse. Now, in the advent of no-fault divorce, adultery is not considered in the breakdown of a marriage and no one has any idea what the verb fornicate means.

SAM: I haven't heard of it.

GRANT: I'm something of a word nerd. I like etymology; knowing the origin of a word provides a deeper insight into what that term is trying to communicate. In Latin, the term fornix means arch or vault. In Ancient Rome, prostitutes waited for their customers out of the rain under arched structures. Fornix became a euphemism for brothels. Curb crawling wasn't a thing back then as there were no cars. Fornicate as an adjective is still used in botany, meaning 'arched' or 'bending over.' In modern usage, the term fornicate is often replaced with more judgment-neutral terms like premarital sex, extramarital sex, or casual sex. It's not like I'm a Puritan or anything, but the problem is that we've pretty much abandoned standards in this area under the false assumption that giving people (both men and women) more choice about when and whom they have sex with would result in greater freedom and happiness. The argument is meretricious; free love is never free. We tend to forget that with more freedom comes more responsibility. It's a case of being careful what you wish for. While you may not have broken any moral laws you've certainly bent them in this case.

SAM: I never thought of it that way.

GRANT: Why would you? From your perspective you were having fun. Hook-up culture is after all promoted and perpetuated by women. Many modern women think they can sleep around in their twenties and settle down in their thirties. But it doesn't work that way. It turns out that hook-up culture favours a highly select group of men that all women want. What is it they say: 'six feet, six pack, six figures.' It's sad how everything these days can be reduced to a hundred-and-forty-character tweet. Most regular guys that don't meet these criteria are all but invisible to most women; few people draw attention to their feelings of social isolation and sexual frustration. You may have good looks and good game, but you are no match for the legal system, which I can assure you will grind you to a pulp as it has the power to strip you of your liberty and make your life a living hell.

SAM: Yeah, I totally regret that night.

GRANT: Hey, we've all been there, I was young once too. I can't believe I said that, I sound like my dad! The difference here is that your decision to sleep with Nancy is now under the microscope.

SAM: I feel I've been lied to.

GRANT: You have, but it is a lie you wanted to be true. Who doesn't want to believe that having sex with someone has no consequence. But criminal courts are not interested in your beliefs.

SAM: I'm starting to think you're right.

GRANT: It's hard to appreciate just how pervasive the idea of free sex is in our society. The ubiquity of porn is a case in point. Porn invariably creates unrealistic sex expectations. We think we're not doing any harm but we can't separate fantasy from reality and we require more stimulus in order to maintain the same response. Sooner or later we get hooked and on a downward spiral.

SAM: Like an addiction.

GRANT: It's the very definition.

SAM: So what's the solution?

GRANT: For a start, stop watching porn. You'll notice your relationships improve. You'll start seeing women as they really are, rather than what you fantasize them to be. The discipline and self-control will spill over into other areas of your life, your studies, your career. It's not easy, you will have setbacks, but every man has to decide whether he will be a slave or a master of his own sexual desires.

SAM: But what about Nancy, doesn't she have some responsibility here? I can tell you that I'm not the first guy she's been with.

GRANT: Nancy is not on trial. Even if she was in the witness box, I can't ask her about her sexual history to impeach her credibility. The are very few downsides to a false allegation of rape in the criminal justice system.

SAM: That's not right. She gets to completely upend my life and there's no consequence for her.

GRANT: Tell me a situation in our society where women are held completely accountable for the consequences of their actions? There's a new Taylor Swift song that recently came out — 'Anti-hero.' There's a line in that song about her looking at the sun but never in the mirror. This is very true of women of today. There are so many safety nets in place, they think they are invincible. Either the government will bail them out or some loser guy will. Everyone loses in this game.

SAM: So that's it?

GRANT: No, not exactly. Mother Nature always yields to Father Time.

Shallow women make the mistake of thinking that their beauty will last forever. A lot of women simply go nuts without male attention. The feminists that complained about the objectifying nature of the male gaze, now complain that men are no longer asking them out. There is a lot of loneliness coming and the pandemic has only made things worse.

SAM: I get it. It's like role reversal. My friend Greg, who is a total tool, is getting DMs from girls he used to troll.

GRANT: You can't blame women for their nature. You can try to understand it and conduct yourself accordingly. There have been a lot of subtle effects of allowing women's feelings to become the arbiter of objective truth in our society. Practically everyone jumped on the Me Too movement with the Harvey Weinstein scandal. I'm not saying that guys like Weinstein and Bill Cosby don't deserve to be punished. They most certainly do. But these days you can hardly say hello to a woman without being accused of sexual harassment.

SAM: I know. Things have become so lame now.

GRANT: Well not for guys like you, that are prepared to break the social rules. Unfortunately, you had a bad break here. The real problem is not the Weinsteins of the world. They are easy to deal with once they are identified. It's when the average Joe doesn't want to play anymore that women will really suffer.

SAM: Why is that?

GRANT: Jordan Peterson with his lobster analogy demonstrated that social hierarchies have persisted since prehistoric times. At the top of any human hierarchy you will find a man. You can choose to ignore this fundamental reality, you can socially engineer your policy to flatten the differences between genders, but what you will end up with is Bruce Jenner transitioning to Caitlyn and becoming *Time*'s Woman of the Year.

SAM: Damn. I never thought about that. But there's still no solution that I can see.

GRANT: The idea that the world would be better if women were in charge will always be with us. This toxic feminism is not unlike the COVID-19 virus. You have to socially distance in order to break the chain of infection.

SAM: I've certainly learned my lesson.

GRANT: I'm sure you have. Anyway, I'm running late. We can follow up by phone.

SAM: Thanks, Grant. I appreciate your help.

GRANT: No problem. Take care.

DIALOGUE 6

Artificial Intelligence

Prior to the Enlightenment it was considered self-evident that there existed a transcendent creator — God. The study of His Word in The Holy Bible was aimed at revealing His glory. The rise of secularism and the concomitant fall of religion resulted in a belief that humans were not the result of Divine Will but rather physical processes. The philosophy of Nietzsche and Darwin's theory of natural selection did much to undermine a faith in God and rationalize the system of laws. In this dialogue, two vampires of the Seculari, Noah and Lewis, discuss secularism in relation to recent developments in Artificial Intelligence. Their dialogue centres on whether the metaphor of artificial intelligence in law, policy and regulatory discussions stems from a secular intellectual hubris — that Man can use science to manipulate nature, defy God, cheat death and achieve immortality. Or whether artificial intelligence is the catalyst for the next step in human evolution — Transhumanism.

NOAH: How are you, Lewis?

LEWIS: Well. Did you hear that business about Anthony?

NOAH: I was on his review committee. He had to go. He presented a danger to all of us.

LEWIS: No doubt. Still, it's a shame. He had such promise.

NOAH: True. Talent is latent potential, maybe that's why the word talent and latent are anagrams. No matter, vampires, like people, waste talent all the time.

LEWIS: Every vampire struggles with eternity.

NOAH: Yes, humans have an existential problem diametrically opposed to our own; they struggle with their own mortality.

LEWIS: Indeed, becoming like us is a fate worse than death. No longer able to reflect the image of God, they will be just like us, not be able to see their own reflection in the mirror.

NOAH: Quite so. We are as Nietzsche might put it, beyond good and evil. However, our lives have no meaning beyond the insatiable thirst for blood.

LEWIS: Wretched thirst. If only they knew what life without death was really like, they wouldn't seek to obtain it.

NOAH: Yes. They were told to seek first the Kingdom of God and His righteousness by the one who shed his own blood for them. They were promised that all things would be added, including eternity. Why didn't they listen?

LEWIS: Why didn't we? Man has a need to control his destiny; he would rather become like God rather than obey and seek to imitate Him.

NOAH: It's an old story. As old as the Tower of Babel.

LEWIS: A city with a tower that reaches the heavens.

NOAH: Right. Once built, nothing would be impossible for Man. But Man is not God, but rather made in the image of God.

LEWIS: When its hubris reaches the heavens, high tech towers are bound to topple under the weight of their own conceit. The operation of technology enlarges output given the same input; this is what most people refer to as efficiency. However, technology also creates its own obsolescence and the creative destruction militates societal trends that are increasingly precipitous. Consider the developments around artificial intelligence.

NOAH: Whatever do you mean? I think the humans are making great progress.

LEWIS: All progress has an endpoint. Here the goal would appear to be the realization of an immortal mind.

NOAH: What's wrong with that?

LEWIS: It is an unending quest, however all efforts to become immortal are idolatrous.

NOAH: How so?

LEWIS: It's rebellion against God, like worshiping a statue or any created thing.

NOAH: Nonsense!

LEWIS: Metaphors convey deeper truth both in science and in literature, they are used all the time. Consider the Big Bang or a heart of stone. The fact that idioms are not literal is unimportant, it's the underlying meaning that is to be examined. Artificial intelligence is a metaphor that suggests human intelligence can be modelled in a generalized sense.

NOAH: And you're saying it can't?

LEWIS: There are tremendous benefits to AI when the problem is well-defined and limited to the performance of a single task such as medical diagnosis, driving a car or the recognition of patterns in large data sets. The problem comes when we worship the technology we have made. Technology is the new religion these days. It tantalizingly holds the prospect of transcendence of the suffering to which all flesh is heir. We overestimate our abilities and are quick to deify our own creation and humbly bow before it in a collective act of genuflection. We say that the algorithm is a 'black-box,' that provides the answer. Artificial intelligence that claims to rival human intelligence is as garish as porn is to sex. It's a caricature, not the real thing. Why does man want that which God created to be man-made? To render that which is infinite, finite? Is it not because man is perennially dissatisfied with his finitude? Human attempts to collapse heaven and earth invariably will create hell on earth.

NOAH: So you have a problem with man improving or upgrading

himself? Should they just have remained in their caves?

LEWIS: No, but there is a fundamental difference between seeking to reveal God's glory and claiming it as your own.

NOAH: I'm not sure what you mean. Every field of human knowledge is evolving. Does it not follow that humans evolve too? I'm all for it.

LEWIS: It is hard to underestimate the profound impact that Darwin has had on the system of research, education and patterns of thought. Universities treat natural selection and the theory of evolution as if they were immutable laws. But any worldview that undermines faith will invariably reduce the individual to that which can be socially constructed.

NOAH: But surely the evidence for Darwin's theory is both over-whelming and uncontroversial at this point. What's wrong with individuals optimizing their lives and engaging in continuous self-improvement?

LEWIS: What you call self-improvement, is more often than not self-deception. We, being evil, crave blood, because it is life and life is good. In the modern age self-righteousness and individualism has replaced seeking to have a right relationship with God.

NOAH: Righteousness.

LEWIS: Yes. Because the self is now worshiped and not God. Personal feelings are all that matter. Everyone is on their own life journey. Avoiding hurting another's feelings becomes the goal. Identity politics becomes a form of self-aggrandizement as individuals and their preferred groups seek to replace objective truth with their 'lived experience.' Speech is no longer used to communicate truth, but rather to further the agenda of particular interest groups. All that remains are siloed humans shouting at the wind.

NOAH: I'm not sure I buy that. Human beings have always sought to augment and enhance themselves. The internet for example has collapsed physical distance and made knowledge accessible in a way that has not occurred at any point in history. Artificial Intelligence will accelerate these developments. It's just the next logical phase in human development.

LEWIS: The internet may have resulted in the death of distance. But digital information is a medium that by its nature is ephemeral. Egyptian hieroglyphs inscribed on clay tablets can be read today even though they were written three thousand years ago.

NOAH: So what?

LEWIS: The Egyptian empire could not expand because those clay tablets could not be transported further than the length of The Nile.

NOAH: Isn't it better that information is now far more accessible?

LEWIS: Better for whom? And what? Cultures develop over centuries as a result of localized knowledge. The inexorable convergence of all media that resulted from the technologies of digitization flattened cultures and made content that could be remixed and rendered on interoperable networked systems. This cultural homogenization invariably served corporate interests as electronic communication could be transmitted instantaneously at low cost with perfect fidelity to the original. It goes some way to explain why Apple's market capitalization is greater than the annual GDP of most countries. Individuals find themselves increasingly socially disconnected and polarized into digital factions rather than familial units. Such social groups, like the digital technologies that create them, are amorphous, pliable and vulnerable.

NOAH: Vulnerable to what?

LEWIS: Vampires and the government.

NOAH: Ha, great for us! The governments in the West are premised on democracy. You have a problem with that now?

LEWIS: Democracy is derived from the Greek *dēmokratia*, from *dēmos* 'the people' and *-kratia* 'power, rule.' The problem comes with 'Vox populi, vox Dei.'

NOAH: The voice of the people is the voice of God.

LEWIS: Right, but what people fail to understand is that the riotousness of the crowd is always very close to madness. Jurisprudence in Western civilization has its foundation in the case law system developed in the Jewish and Christian legal traditions. Societies and the laws that govern them invariably reflect the character of the religion and its God. The Rule of Law and inviolability of human rights can be traced to the idea that man was made in the image of God. The legal maxim 'innocent until proven guilty' has its origin, its Genesis, in the idea of Man's divine nature. This divinity afforded him due process protections in law. These laws were later categorized by Blackstone in his commentaries only to be famously dismissed as ancestor wisdom by Bentham.

NOAH: Utilitarianism?

LEWIS: Underpinning all of Bentham's ideas was utilitarianism. It demanded that laws and government should serve 'the greatest good for the greatest number." Bentham argued that the English common law should be codified, although certainly not on any abstract concept of inalienable human rights, an idea he described as 'nonsense on stilts.'

NOAH: But you realize that a short while prior to Bentham the Church was burning people at the stake. The Church was one of the most corrupt institutions then and some would say now. There's a reason that there exists a separation of church and state. Why would you surrender your ability to reason in favour of submitting to an authority over which you have zero control?

LEWIS: Because in the absence of God, the Supreme Court becomes the final court of appeal. As definitive as their judgements might seem, all precedents can ultimately be overturned by subsequent courts. This is not so with God. I have no problem with the separation of church and state. I do have a problem with the separation of morality and state. Without human rights that are inviolable Man becomes infinitely malleable rather than inalienable.

NOAH: So what's the plan? Derive AI regulation from an exegetical account of the Tower of Babel!

LEWIS: Secular reasoning has its place. It just needs to be applied with humility and oriented towards non-secular teleological ends. The policy goal is too short term with its calculus of benefits and harms and set far too low with its ostensible aim of establishing public trust.

NOAH: So policy should be aiming for the Kingdom of God? That's a little vague, don't you think?

LEWIS: Without this fundamental orientation our actions cannot be measured against the standard of truth. Being unable to admit we are wrong, we are left with gerrymandering the evidence to fit the current narrative as defined by the consensus — we obey Demos rather than Deus.

NOAH: OK so what might that standard be?

LEWIS: Not what, who. In the West that person is Christ, for in Him all things are yes and amen. Consider if you will the protagonist Winston in Orwell's *1984*. Winston must love Big Brother before he is allowed to die. He is not permitted to die a martyr as this will only inspire others to follow his example and seek truth. His death absent submission to Big Brother would make him a symbol of resistance to tyranny and that cannot stand. Though he seeks to cling to objective reality he tragically realizes that betrayal by those closest to him is the price of truth. Subjected to physical and psychological torture he comes to really believe that $2 + 2 = 5$. His indoctrination is finally complete when he sincerely declares his love for Big Brother.

NOAH: A most proleptic book. The internet has made it much easier to manipulate the past. It's a lot easier than admitting you were wrong and contending with the truth.

LEWIS: This explains why a man declaring himself to be God incarnate can be betrayed and executed though completely innocent and without a fair trial. Truth, particularly Truth personified, will be offensive to anyone cloaked with deceit. But truth has curative attributes so you have to take on faith that although you may be subject to bodily harm, repentance and belief in Christ is the only path to true forgiveness and redemption.

NOAH: But what about the other religions?

LEWIS: What about the other religions? It's not that they are valueless, but either Christ is who he says he is or all faithful Christians are attempting to imitate the life of a lunatic. But before you throw out baby Jesus with the bathwater, it would be wise to note that religious tolerance and modern science and the current legal system are Christian innovations. The legal jurisprudence of the West would have developed very differently had it been based on Islam. Unmoored from its Christian foundation, human rights are paid lip service in the current Human Rights Code guided by the dimmed fog lights of centuries past.

NOAH: Not sure about that, what about all the wars that have been started in the name of religion?

LEWIS: Just because you're Christian, or follow any other religion for that matter, does not mean you can't also be hypocritical. You may well profess atheism and yet be a highly moral person. You just can't give an adequate account of where your moral behavior comes from. Now it is the case, whatever religion you profess, if you have qualified to practice law in any Western country, you have been grafted onto a legal tree that has Jewish and Christian values at its moral root. You can deny this fact, but you would be sweeping away centuries of historical fact in the process. We seem to have forgotten where our conceptions of human rights came from in much the same way that we have forgotten that New Year's Day marks the circumcision of Christ eight days after the date marking his birth December 25th. This is important because as the existentialist Sartre has noted, no finite point has meaning without an infinite reference point. Much effort has gone into erasing Christ from the public consciousness. But in the inexorable effort to be inclusive we have paradoxically become more intolerant. The secularization of our laws has resulted in an etiolation of legal reasoning and created a society of morally anemic lawyers.

NOAH: You're really kicking the hornet's nest with that one.

LEWIS: Lawyers are human, they lose their way like everyone else. However, in the absence of a Godhead, Christ to whom we can repent and believe, there is no forgiveness of sin. In the absence of objective truth all that matters is who controls the narrative, which will be fashioned to suit whoever happens to be the prevailing interest group. There is no right and wrong, as the moral categories of good and bad have no meaning since truth is whatever you want it to be. Two plus two can equal five. Vampires can be saints.

NOAH: Ah relativism, that immoral tune that keeps on playing.

LEWIS: Yes, but eventually someone has to pay the pied piper; metastasis is an attribute of relativism. It corrodes from within. Truth by contrast is remedial.

NOAH: Yes, there's a reason we avoid light. So what's this all got to do with AI?

LEWIS: If there is no God, then the claims of moral relativism make perfect sense; humans should do whatever they want, it doesn't matter. All that matters is who is in power.

NOAH: Isn't that the very essence of survival of the fittest?

LEWIS: In Darwinian terms vampires are at the apex of the evolutionary pyramid. We have immortality and yet we are unknown to God, our souls are black holes that reflect no good. AI, at least in its most secularized and generalized sense, will seek to replace man's heart with a heart of silicone. Secularist man seeks to live a long life rather than a good life. Following Bentham, individual happiness and happiness for the greatest number will be prioritized over duty to God and to one's neighbor. We, being evil incarnate, have souls that cannot be redeemed. Eternity has been removed from our hearts so we will never be known by the one who knows all.

NOAH: Truly forsaken and blotted out of the book of the living. So what do you think they'll choose, to pick up their cross and follow Jesus or excise the eternity that's been placed in their hearts and be like us?

LEWIS: Well one thing is for sure, there's no way to transcend death without confronting the problem of moral evil. We were there at the beginning. Their attempts to seek immortality will cause them to become as bloodthirsty as we are.

NOAH: Yes. All regimes that have attempted to usher in utopia have had to do so by shedding blood, but democracy has ultimately prevailed.

LEWIS: Are you sure about that? Regardless of the political system, governmental policy can either be realized by coercion, compensation or ideological persuasion. Coercion is the policy measure of choice in totalitarian regimes because there is no higher authority. Totalitarian regimes centralize governmental authority and take Draconian measures to enforce their plans. Democratic regimes have access to the same AI technology as their totalitarian counterparts, power and control will just take different forms. In democracy, with its obeisance to markets, it will be expressed as surveillance capitalism and in dictatorships, with their proclivity towards centralized authority, it will result in state surveillance.

NOAH: It will be different this time. With Dataism as the new religion and AI technology as its catalyst, humans can finally accelerate the slow evolutionary processes. Once they fully map and manipulate the genomic sequences, organisms will be properly understood as biological algorithms, processors of data.

LEWIS: Hackable animals?

NOAH: Exactly. Death is a technical problem with a technical solution.

LEWIS: But that path won't lead them to God, it will lead them to us. Like us, they would have eyes that do not see and ears that do not hear.

NOAH: Transhumanism is the future. The merging of man and machine is inevitable. It's happening now with the metaverse. Virtual reality will eventually become just reality.

LEWIS: But avatars cannot be martyrs; they cannot die for their beliefs. Humans will be far easier to control than they are now. If the Coronavirus pandemic was any indication of people's willingness to surrender their freedoms wholesale to government and big tech, the task will be a facile one. All-knowing transhumans are not the same as wise actual humans.

NOAH: Why is that?

LEWIS: Wisdom and knowledge are the result of very different pedagogical processes. The primary difference between the two is that wisdom involves a perspective and context and the ability to make discerning judgments about a subject. Anyone or anything can become knowledgeable about a subject by reading, researching, and memorizing facts. AI and technology accelerate the accumulation and processing of knowledge, but without wisdom they will both amplify and intensify the worst of human nature.

NOAH: That would explain how porn drove the development of the internet. So where do you think this will all end?

LEWIS: It will end, as the poets say, at the beginning. After all the exploration we will arrive where we started and know the place for the first time through the unknown, unremembered gate. The few that now see in the mirror dimly, will know fully as they are fully known.

NOAH: And what about the rest — the ones that persist in the pursuit of the immortal mind through AI technologies?

LEWIS: They will look into the black mirror and see us.

Selected Readings

DIALOGUE 1 — THE TWO-BODY HIRE

Sowell, T. (2009). *Black rednecks & white liberals*. Encounter Books.

Sowell, T. (2012). *Intellectuals and society*. Hachette UK.

Commons, J. R. (1931). 'Institutional economics.' *The American economic review*, 648-657.

Lukianoff, G., & Haidt, J. (2019). *The coddling of the American mind: how good intentions and bad ideas are setting up a generation for failure*. New York City: Penguin Books.

DIALOGUE 2 — THE LIBRARY ARCHIVE

Johnson, P. E. (2010). *Darwin on trial*. InterVarsity Press.

Craig, W. L. (2008). *Reasonable faith: Christian truth and apologetics*. Crossway.

Girard, R. (1976). *Deceit, desire, and the novel: self and other in literary structure*. Baltimore: Johns Hopkins University Press.

Kuhn, T. S. (2012). *The structure of scientific revolutions*. University of Chicago Press.

DIALOGUE 3 — THE ABORTION

Roe v. Wade, 410 U.S. 113 (1973)

R v Morgentaler, (1988) 1 SCR 30

Dobbs v. Jackson Women's Health Organization, 597 U.S. ___ (2022)

Dialogue 4 — Student Life

Ovid, & Mandelbaum, A. (1995). *The Metamorphoses of Ovid: a new verse translation by Allen Mandelbaum.* (1st Harvest ed.). San Diego: Harcourt Brace.

Phillips, K. M. (1968). 'Perseus and Andromeda.' *American Journal of Archaeology,* 72(1), 1–23.

Dialogue 5 — Trial Prep

Fiamengo, Janice (2017). *Sons of feminism: men have their say.* Little Nightingale Press.

Mulvey, L. (1989). 'Visual pleasure and narrative cinema.' In *Visual and other pleasures* (pp. 14-26). London: Palgrave Macmillan UK.

Dialogue 6 — Artificial Intelligence

Lennox, J. C. (2020). *2084: Artificial intelligence and the future of humanity.* Zondervan.

Harari, Y. N. (2016). *Homo Deus: A brief history of tomorrow.* Random House.

www.ingramcontent.com/pod-product-compliance
Lightning Source LLC
Chambersburg PA
CBHW070457220526
45466CB00004B/1858